INTRODUCTION

Risk is everywhere—driving in traffic, breathing city air, expressing your views. Add decisions about what career to pursue, whom to marry, where to live, when to change jobs—and it's clear: risk is unavoidable.

Avoiding one risk often backs us into another. While eliminating nuclear power would avoid related radioactive accidents, burning more fossil fuel would increase acid rain and the ''greenhouse effect'' on climate.

The issue for people in business is not whether to take risks, but how to take reasonable risks. Business risks often have broad impacts that affect customers, employees, shareholders, suppliers, and/or community residents. Decision makers in government have even broader influence on issues of peace, justice, the economy, disease control, and international trade.

How you handle risk affects your career and your personal growth. How we collectively handle risk affects our organizational success and societal well-being.

OVERVIEW

This book presents a systematic three-phase process for making decisions in risky situations. It addresses the important questions raised during each phase. These questions are summarized below and elaborated in the following pages.

I. DIAGNOSIS

1. What are your *objectives* in this situation?
2. What *alternative paths* are likely to lead to your objectives? How can each be evaluated?
3. Is your decision likely to be colored by your personal *risk-taking tendencies*?

II. PLANNING AND PREPARATION

4. What *type of change* is appropriate to this situation: incremental or transformational?
5. What *decision process* serves the needs of the stakeholders: unilateral, bargaining, decision rule, or collaborative?
6. How can you gain the most favorable *reward/risk ratio*: more information and control, less exposure to potential loss?

III. IMPLEMENTATION

7. How can you overcome common *risk-taking barriers,* such as miscalculating moral consequences, overreacting to pressure, and failing to use available information?
8. Is a small-scale trial feasible? What outcomes should be monitored? Are corrections needed? What can be learned?

RISK TAKING

A Guide For Decision Makers

Herbert S. Kindler, Ph.D.

CRISP PUBLICATIONS, INC.
Los Altos, California

RISK TAKING
A Guide For Decision Makers

Herbert S. Kindler, Ph.D.

Cover Photo: George Fiske (1835-1918)
Half Dome and Glacier Point, Yosemite Valley
c. 1880, Albumen print, 10 × 7 in.
The Oakland Museum Founders Fund
From the exhibition *Picturing California: A Century of Photographic Genius*
organized by The Oakland Museum

CREDITS
Editors: **Tony Hicks and Michael Crisp**
Designer: **Carol Harris**
Typesetting: **Interface Studio**
Cover Design: **Carol Harris**
Artwork: **Ralph Mapson**

Copyright © 1990 by Crisp Publications, Inc.
Printed in the United States of America

Crisp books are distributed in Canada by Reid Publishing, Ltd., P.O. Box 7267, Oakville, Ontario, Canada L6J 6L6.

In Australia by Career Builders, P.O. Box 1051, Springwood, Brisbane, Queensland, Australia 4127.

And in New Zealand by Career Builders, P.O. Box 571, Manurewa, New Zealand.

Library of Congress Catalog Card Number 89-81247
Kindler, Herbert S.
Risk Taking
ISBN 0-931961-76-9

PREFACE

The purpose of this book is to help you think about how you currently deal with situations involving risk and explore how you might manage risk more effectively.

Publisher Mike Crisp suggested this book be written because the need to make decisions involving risk arises daily in the organizational world—yet little guidance is available to the decision maker.

Perhaps the risk-taking literature is so sparse because the topic embraces two highly disparate bodies of knowledge: *decision theory* and *human behavior*.

This book takes on the challenge of bridging these knowledge foundations with a structure accessible and useful to decision makers at all organizational levels.

Specifically, this book is designed to help you:

- Manage risky decisions with a systematic framework

- Learn more about your own willingness to take risks

- Handle risk with more awareness, skill, and assurance

To get the full rewards, please risk completing the exercises that appear throughout the text. The book can be used by groups as a training program or by individuals for self-study.

Herb Kindler

ABOUT THE AUTHOR

HERBERT S. KINDLER, Ph.D., conducts training programs for organizations with diverse risk-taking cultures, including ARCO, BBDO, Hughes Aircraft Company, IBM, JVC, McDonnell Douglas, Mercedes Benz, Navistar, Northrop, TRW, and the U.S. Navy.

His organizational experience includes the positions of chief engineer and chief executive officer. Dr. Kindler graduated from MIT and received his doctorate in management from UCLA.

As director of the Center for Management Effectiveness, he provides management seminars and consulting services in the United States and abroad. As professor of management at Loyola Marymount University in Los Angeles, he teaches managerial skill development. He is listed in *Who's Who in America*.

Dr. Kindler welcomes comments from readers and can be reached at: The Center for Management Effectiveness, P.O. Box 1202, Pacific Palisades, CA 90272. (213) 459-6052.

ACKNOWLEDGMENTS

Marilyn Ginsburg, M.F.C.C., psychotherapist in private practice, helped significantly in the book's conceptual development.

Mike Crisp, in addition to suggesting the need for this book, added to its readability through his editing contributions.

Other individuals who provided insightful comments and helpful suggestions are:

David Boje, Ph.D., Associate Professor, College of Business Administration, Loyola Marymount University

Francisco Coronel, Ph.D., Associate Professor, College of Business Administration, Loyola Marymount University

Jeanne Hartley, Director, Employee Relations and Development, Centinela Hospital Medical Center

Eric Herzog, Ph.D., President, Optimum Performance Systems

Frank Wagner, Ph.D., Partner, Prism, Ltd.

CONTENTS

YOU CAN'T AVOID RISK

By Lee Lorenz, reprinted from *The New Yorker* with permission.

GUIDING PRINCIPLES

As you consider accepting a risk, keep four principles in mind:

1. *Learning and personal growth require taking risks.*

A life lived to maintain security, by holding onto the status quo, eventually becomes a prison. Personal development requires loosening your grip on what you already have mastered and moving beyond your ''comfort zone'' into the unknown.

2. *Take only those risks where you can handle the loss.*

All risky situations can result in loss. In a worst-case scenario, if the loss would be catastrophic (materially or emotionally), don't take the risk *in its present form.*

To build self-confidence, start small. Don't begin by plunging into risks with heavy penalties. As you gain experience, harsh choices often become less burdensome. For example, putting your job on the line is less stressful after you've already made some successful career changes.

3. *Adjust risks that are too much of a gamble.*

Consider improving the odds and reducing the chances of loss by obtaining more information, spreading the liability, hedging your bet, and gaining more control over the outcome of your decision.

4. *Accept that the price of risking is occasional failure.*

Don't demand a perfect track record of yourself or others. One employee put $100,000 at risk in a promotional campaign. When she sheepishly told her boss about the negative outcome, the boss asked what she had learned from the experience. In surprise she asked, ''Do you mean I'm not fired?'' ''How could I even think of firing you?'' the boss said. ''I've just invested $100,000 in your education!''

I

Diagnosis

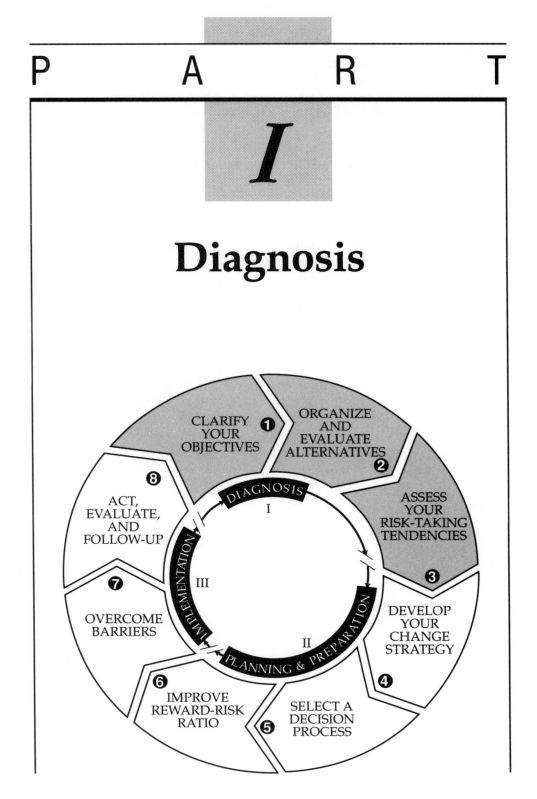

PART I. DIAGNOSIS

The starting point for risk-taking is getting clear about your goals. Where do you want your career to go? What projects are important to you? What do you want from your relationships? Your vision of what really matters will help you decide which risks to take, which to modify, and which to skip.

A central fact of risk-taking is that you don't know the outcome beforehand. Risk-takers are explorers—they open new territory and take a chance on losing their stake if they fail.

There are two basic approaches to every risky situation. One is the more *conservative approach*, with a track record and a high-probability outcome. The other requires that you loosen your hold on what feels secure and reach for something that could open fresh possibilities. The outcome of this more *risky alternative* is cloaked in uncertainty, and there's a possibility that you might find yourself worse off. The terms *conservative* and *risky* are relative and descriptive, not absolute and judgmental. Either type of alternative is appropriate under certain circumstances, which we will examine in detail. Our definition of risk:

> *Risk is a course of action or inaction, taken under conditions of uncertainty, which exposes one to possible loss in order to reach a desired outcome.*

The possible loss is of two kinds: the outcome may leave decision makers worse off than before (*a real loss*); or the outcome may be less favorable than it might have been (*an opportunity loss*).

The diagnostic phase consists of three steps: (1) clarify the objectives you want to achieve; (2) structure the alternative paths to your objectives so that you can evaluate them; and (3) recognize your own risk-taking bias.

To relate these steps to situations you might encounter, three scenarios are presented. After each situation, answer the diagnostic questions.

ALPHA OR OMEGA?

You must decide whether to replace an existing product, Alpha, with a new product, Omega. The radical new Omega design, according to its advocates in R&D, will make Alpha obsolete overnight. Your marketing pros estimate a 70 percent chance of strong consumer acceptance for Omega. If this happens, they predict that profits will increase to $62 million a year. But if consumer acceptance turns out to be weak (a 30 percent chance), they predict that profits will decline to $5 million a year. In this case, the original product could not be reintroduced for at least three years.

If you decide to continue selling the still viable Alpha, with only minor refinements to give it a somewhat fresh look, you have a 96 percent chance of continuing its current profits of $45 million a year. There is a 4 percent chance that Alpha will meet tougher competition and profits will decline to $40 million a year.

Based on accepting the available information and estimates as accurate, would you launch innovative Omega during the coming year, or would you stay with tried-and-true Alpha? Please check your response.

1. ____ I would continue to market Alpha.

2. ____ I lean toward continuing to market Alpha, but without conviction.

3. ____ I could go either way (market either Alpha or Omega).

4. ____ I lean toward replacing Alpha with Omega, but without conviction.

5. ____ I would replace Alpha with Omega.

Before helping you interpret your scoring, consider two other risky situations.

DIAGNOSIS (Continued)

SMALL IS BEAUTIFUL

Your company has earned consistent profits by bidding only on small construction projects. An opportunity develops to land a really large contract. Because of your firm's low overhead, you estimate a 60 percent chance of winning the large project and achieving a $300,000 profit during the coming year. But you will have to divert a lot of time and talent from your traditional marketing efforts. If you fail to win the contract (a 40 percent chance), your annual profit will drop to $126,000 during the coming year. Your current business strategy has a 96 percent chance of continuing to yield a $230,000 annual profit, with a 4 percent chance of dropping to $210,000.

Please check your preference.

1. _____ I would continue to bid only on small contracts.

2. _____ I would lean toward bidding only on small contracts, but without conviction.

3. _____ I could go either way (bid only on small contracts, or bid on the large job and fewer small contracts).

4. _____ I would lean toward bidding on the large construction project and fewer small contracts, but without conviction.

5. _____ I would bid on the large construction project and fewer small contracts.

SMALL IS BEAUTIFUL

FIGHT OR SETTLE

Your company is being sued for $500,000 because your new product design allegedly infringes another firm's patent. The issue is not clearcut, and your legal team estimates you have a 55 percent chance of winning the case. The losing party must pay all legal and court costs, amounting to $55,000. The other company is willing to drop the suit for an out-of-court settlement of $255,000. If you agree to an out-of-court settlement, you have a 10 percent chance of bargaining the settlement figure down to $200,000.

Please indicate your preferred action.

1. ____ I would take the out-of-court settlement.

2. ____ I would lean toward taking the out-of-court settlement.

3. ____ I could go either way (either settle out of court, or fight the lawsuit).

4. ____ I would lean toward fighting the lawsuit.

5. ____ I would fight the lawsuit.

The first three steps of any risk-taking situation should be diagnostic. Starting on the following page, notice how each step adds focus to the risks imbedded in the scenarios you have just reviewed.

STEP 1: CLARIFY YOUR OBJECTIVES

Goal clarity helps you assign weights to alternative action in risky situations.

The value of goal clarity can be seen in a decision aimed at reducing risk at Schumberger, Ltd. This French industrial giant dominates the oilfield service business that it pioneered. During the 1970's, the company accrued large profits when oil production and exploration boomed. Management decided to diversify into electronics to protect its profits from oil-industry swings by buying Fairchild in 1979. Despite pumping billions into this semiconductor manufacturer, operating losses mounted. In 1987, Fairchild was sold at the bargain price of $122 million. Schumberger's diversification decision was not guided by the objective of ''sticking to its knitting'' (which Peters and Waterman attributed to Schlumberger in their 1982 best-selling book, *In Search of Excellence*). Instead of seeking other ways to hedge or buffer profits from oil-industry fluctuations, Schlumberger actually *increased* its risk by entering an industry in which management had little experience.

Before deciding on a course of action, identify your organization's top priorities. For example, in the *Alpha* or *Omega* case, you might re-examine the firm's business plan. If a rapid increase in market share is the goal, you would more seriously consider the risky alternative—launch Omega. If your company's objective is modest, stable growth that doesn't put employees' jobs in jeopardy, you would give more weight to the conservative option— continue to market Alpha.

STEP 2: ORGANIZE AND EVALUATE ALTERNATIVES

In the first two preceding scenarios, the "risky" decision seeks a new gain, with the possibility of a significant loss. The "conservative" decision seeks to maintain the status quo, with the probability of no more than a slight loss or setback.

Figure 1 shows the two types of options in the *Alpha* or *Omega* scenario in a decision-tree format.

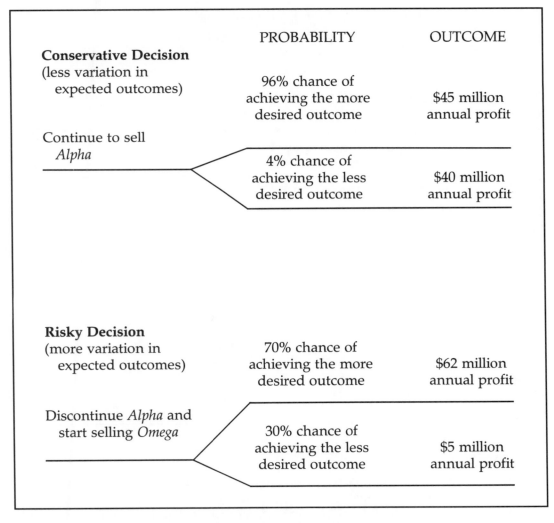

Figure 1. Alpha or Omega Decision Tree

STEP 2: ORGANIZE AND EVALUATE ALTERNATIVES (Continued)

The purpose of using a decision tree is to organize information so you can easily calculate the *expected value* of each decision.

> *Expected value is a measure of the gain (or loss) that you anticipate from a decision outcome.*
>
> *Expected value is calculated by multiplying the* **probability** *of the outcome by the amount of the gain (or loss) that the outcome would bring.*

The expected values of the *Alpha or Omega* decisions are calculated in Figure 2. Expected values can be calculated only for outcomes that can be expressed numerically. In other cases, when a human life, dignity, morale, or an aesthetic issue is at risk, descriptive comparisons should be used.

DECISION	PROBABILITY		OUTCOME		
Continue to sell Alpha (conservative decision)	.96	×	$45 million	=	$43.2 million
	.04	×	$40 million	=	$ 1.6 million
					$44.8 million Expected Value
Launch Omega (risky decision)	.70	×	$62 million	=	$43.4 million
	.30	×	$ 5 million	=	$ 1.5 million
					$44.9 million Expected Value

Figure 2. Alpha-Omega Expected Values

One way to decide between two alternatives is to select the alternative with the highest expected value. However, in the *Alpha or Omega* example, the total is about the same for both alternatives. In fact, all three scenarios are designed with equal expected values for both alternatives. (For *Small Is Beautiful* the expected value for each alternative is close to $230,000. For *Fight or Settle* the expected value for each alternative is about −$250,000.)

STEP 3: ASSESS YOUR RISK-TAKING TENDENCIES

Your reactions to the three preceding scenarios offer clues to your risk-propensity pattern, or how you respond to risky situations in general. To examine these clues, turn back to your answers for each scenario. Transfer the numbers you checked to the ''scoreboard'' below.

RISK-TENDENCY SCOREBOARD

Scenario #1: *Alpha or Omega?*
> Alpha, with conviction = 1; Probably Alpha = 2; Either way = 3; Probably Omega = 4; Omega, with conviction = 5
>
> YOUR SCORE _____

Scenario #2: *Small Is Beautiful?*
> Small contracts, with conviction = 1; Probably small contracts = 2; Either way = 3; Probably large contracts = 4; Large contracts, with conviction = 5
>
> YOUR SCORE _____

Scenario #3: *Fight Or Settle?*
> Settle out-of-court, with conviction = 1; Probably settle out-of-court = 2; Either way = 3; Probably fight in court = 4; Fight in court, with conviction = 5
>
> YOUR SCORE _____

SCORING INTERPRETATION

- Where you scored 1, a conservative or *risk-avoiding preference* is indicated. That is, even though the facts of the case are neutral, you felt strongly that you wanted to maintain the status quo.

- Where you scored 2, 3, or 4, you reveal a tendency to be *risk neutral*. Your decision is based purely on the objective facts; you are not biased either toward or away from risks.

- Where you scored 5, you indicate a *risk-seeking preference*.

STEP 3: ASSESS YOUR RISK-TAKING TENDENCIES (Continued)

Some people score the Fight or Settle scenario differently from the other situations. The first two cases offer *opportunities*; the *Fight or Settle* scenario presents a *threat*. In a threatening situation, one faces a loss potential without the possibility of improving one's current position. An opportunity, on the other hand, offers payoffs that can improve the status quo. Is your pattern of response different with an opportunity than with a threat?

Interestingly, research shows that more people are risk-seeking under threat of a sure loss, particularly where large sums of money are involved. For example, most people would risk a 50 percent chance of losing $10,000, rather than accepting a sure loss of $5,000. Holloway suggests that people reason: "If I can break even, I will get back to the status quo, and that's important to me."* Brazerman explains: "Many individuals may be risk-seeking regarding large losses to avoid being labeled a loser."**

In taking risks, it's important to know what personal orientation you bring to each risky situation. Three scenarios are too small a sample to be definitive. Rather, they are intended to be provocative, to encourage you to focus attention on your tendency to seek either *security* or *stimulation* in your life. As you heighten self-awareness, you can decide how far your bias—for or against risk taking—colors your decisions.

Appropriate risk taking is fundamental to organizational success and personal satisfaction. Risk taking enables us to add zest to our lives, challenge to our work, and opportunity to our careers. Risk taking fuels creativity. Heroes are people who take risks—explorers, astronauts, intellectual pioneers—who, by venturing into the unknown, reduce the fear of uncertainty for others. Risk taking sets the stage for stimulating adventure, competitive advantage, and personal development. The risk of being vulnerable with others makes intimacy, caring, and love possible.

> *Risk involves exposing yourself to discomfort or loss for the sake of moving beyond present limitations*

---

* C. Holloway, *Decision Making Under Uncertainty*, Englewood Cliffs, N.J.: Prentice-Hall, 1979.
** M. H. Brazerman, *Judgment In Managerial Decision Making*, New York: Wiley, 1986.

YOU TRY IT!

Risk taking can be pushed too far. It can become a pattern of thrill seeking and high drama.

Because risking is not always appropriate, use your planning-and-preparation phase to choose which risks to take, which to adjust, and which to skip. Before reviewing this second phase of risk taking, identify a *real situation* where you have to make important choices under conditions of uncertainty.

YOUR SCENARIO

1. Briefly describe a problem situation involving risk that concerns you.

   _____

   _____

   _____

   _____

   _____

2. With respect to this situation, indicate your principal objective.

   _____

   _____

   _____

   _____

3. Identify alternative options that could lead to your objective or help resolve your problem.

   (a) _____

   _____

   _____

   _____

   (b) _____

   _____

   _____

   _____

YOU TRY IT! (Continued)

3. (c) _____

_____

_____

_____

(d) _____

_____

_____

_____

4. For each course of action describe the expected value (if it can be quantitatively expressed): potential benefits and potential negative consequences.

(a) _____

_____

_____

_____

_____

(b) _____

_____

_____

_____

_____

4. (c) _____

_____

_____

_____

_____

(d) _____

_____

_____

_____

_____

As you evaluate alternatives, are you being unduly influenced by a high need for security or for excitement? If you detect a bias toward risk avoiding or risk seeking, consider: Is it appropriate to this situation? Is it counter-productive? Is it fair to other stakeholders?

II

Planning and Preparation

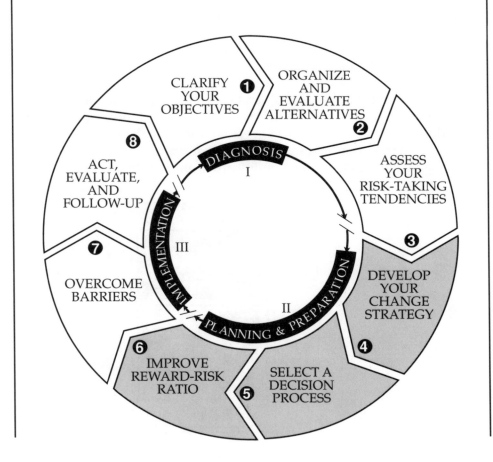

STEP 4: DEVELOP YOUR CHANGE STRATEGY

Risk occurs at transition times—when you must decide between continuing the current system or changing it. To take appropriate risks, you need to understand the *type of change* that fits each situation.

A. Identify Available Strategies

Two fundamental types of change-planning strategies are available to you: *incremental* and *transformational*. Both are required for organizational renewal and personal growth.

Incremental change is step-by-step movement along a well-worn path, representing *variations in degree* within an existing framework. It is based on precedent and aims at doing more of the same, only better.

An incremental change strategy is appropriate when (1) the present system is adequate to support the planners' current objectives, (2) the system and its environment appear stable—for example, no dramatic changes have occurred in technology, competition, or government regulation, and (3) a backlog of incremental-change possibilities is available whose benefits outweigh their costs.

Transformational change is a *variation in kind* rather than in degree. New concepts or assumptions are needed for transformational change. It results in a new way of doing things and requires a creative leap of faith. The risk—moving from the known to the unknown—is worth considering once you decide that incremental change will no longer take you toward your objectives.

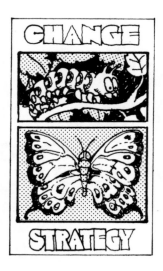

A. Identify Available Strategies (Continued)

All change meets with some resistance—ranging from sincere doubt about the feasibility, benefits, or timing of the change, to fears of losing one's security or influence. Transformational change meets with added resistance because it involves a new and fundamentally different way of doing things. Therefore, when you decide on a transformational strategy, you need to develop a plan to overcome the added resistance. Also, be aware that with a new frame of reference, outcome probabilities will be imprecise estimates.

In the diagnosis phase, you identified alternative paths to your objectives. Now, determine whether each alternative represents an incremental or a transformational change.

| | TYPE OF CHANGE (Incremental or |
| ALTERNATIVE COURSES OF ACTION | Transformational) |

(a) _____   _____

_____

_____

_____

_____

(b) _____   _____

_____

_____

_____

_____

STEP 4: DEVELOP YOUR CHANGE
STRATEGY (Continued)

ALTERNATIVE COURSES OF ACTION

TYPE OF CHANGE
(Incremental or
Transformational)

(c) _____   _____

_____

_____

_____

_____

(d) _____   _____

_____

_____

_____

_____

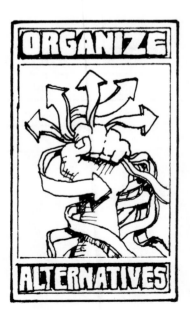

B. Select the Appropriate Strategy

If no one alternative stands out as the most desirable, start with an incremental strategy; it is more likely to be supported by those who must implement it. However, a series of incremental changes can have diminishing returns. Eventually, a crisis will arise. Then transformational change can be the lever to open new opportunities. The following situation illustrates this sequential approach.

> A city's roadway system handled its transportation needs well. Incremental changes, such as adding lanes and straightening curves, were adequate for a while. However, as the town grew, a (transformational) traffic regulation policy became necessary. Within this regulatory framework, such incremental changes as tolls, metered access, and carpool lanes proved effective—again, for awhile. The city council and business leaders are now developing a new (transformational) "telecommuting" approach. They plan to reward organizations whose employees reduce commute traffic by working with computer terminals and fax machines from their homes.

Notice how each new transformational policy makes possible a series of new incremental changes. At some point, every policy or system becomes less responsive to change and, in fact, prevents further growth. That's when a new system, process, design, or underlying assumption is needed to keep the path to your objectives open. Figure 3 (on next page) illustrates how this transformational-incremental-transformational approach avoids a permanent sales plateau for the Alpha product.

STEP 4: DEVELOP YOUR CHANGE STRATEGY (Continued)

B. SELECT THE APPROPRIATE STRATEGY (Continued)

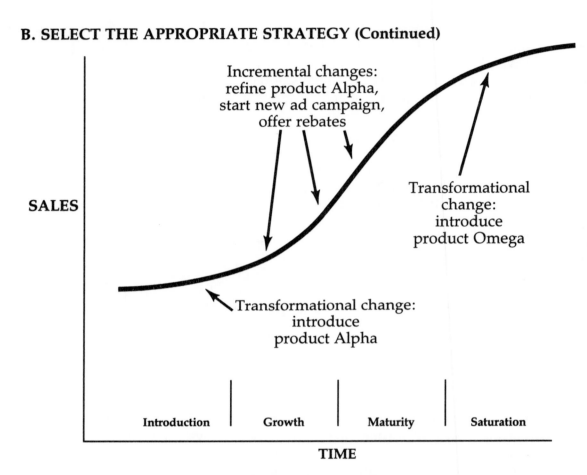

Figure 3. Life Cycle for Alpha

The S-shaped curve is characteristic of all organic systems. For example, if a male and female fruit fly are placed in a glass jar under supportive conditions, after getting acquainted, they multiply exponentially until the jar is too full for further growth.

In Figure 3, sales start to grow slowly after the transformational introduction of product Alpha. As long as the market isn't saturated, incremental changes—such as refining the product design, offering new optional features, or providing rebates—can be effective. At the top of the S-curve, however, saturation is reached and only a transformational change can increase the sales level further. At this point, if continued sales growth is desired, company executives must risk transformational change.

STEP 5: SELECT A DECISION PROCESS

Organizational folklore portrays the manager as a decision gunslinger. Faced with a choice, the hero-manager—with one finger on the trigger—moves in and quickly resolves a tough issue. But with uncertainty, ambiguity, and multiple stakeholders, decisions rarely lend themselves to swift, unilateral action. Before deciding about a risky situation, it's crucial to choose an appropriate decision *process*.

The decision process should (1) lead to solving the problem, (2) gain acceptance of the people who must implement the decision, (3) satisfy time constraints, and (4) provide benefits that outweigh the costs.

Four decision processes are available:

Unilateral—one person has sole decision-making responsibility

Collaboration—a group decision brings together the views of two or more people

Bargaining—two parties arrive at a decision by making offers and counter-offers

Decision Rule—two or more people agree to reach a decision by an objective method such as a vote, lottery, or formula (calculating expected value, for example)

More information about these four processes is provided in Figures 4 and 5, shown on the next two pages.

Test yourself. Select a decision process for each of the four situations that follow on pages 26 and 27. In each case, choose the process that best achieves the results you want: *quality, acceptance, timeliness,* and *cost effectiveness.* Assume you are personally involved in each scenario. Assume also that all participants in each situation are competent to handle the decision-making process you select. Circle only one decision process. If you would use two or more sequentially, circle the *last* process, the one that sets the course of action.

Figure 4. Decision Process Inventory

DECISION PROCESS	DECISION PROCESS EXAMPLE (judicial)	DEFINITION OF DECISION PROCESS
UNILATERAL	judge decides	The **unilateral** process occurs when an individual exercises his or her sole *judgment* in deciding between alternative possibilities. The decision is made when the action to be taken, or not taken, is communicated. Before reaching a unilateral decision, the decision maker may consult others, conduct surveys, organize adversarial debate, or otherwise prepare for exercising his or her judgment.
BARGAINING	plea bargaining by attorneys	**Bargaining** is a process of seeking an agreement in which each party tries to settle what course of action each shall pursue. It is a transaction in which each party seeks a zone of agreement in which to maximize gains and minimize concessions. The decision is an agreement to compromise, trade off, or take turns. It is reached during the process of *mutual adjustment* when the offer of one party is accepted by the other.
COLLABORATION	jury decides	**Collaboration** is a collective process that produces a group decision. The process requires sensitive, respectful attention to the concerns of all participants. It attempts to bring together all informed, relevant views without disregarding any. Collaboration seeks a synergy that serves the needs of all participants. Unanimity is desirable but not essential; a decision is reached when the ''sense of the meeting'' or ''collective view'' is expressed in terms that are generally acceptable.
DECISION RULE	vote by supreme court justices	In the **decision-rule** process, participants accept an *outside element* as the basis for deciding among predetermined alternatives. That is, after the alternative courses of action have been defined, the decision rule is used to choose among them. Any of the preceding decision processes may be used to select options and to select which decision rule to apply. The rule may be a voting procedure, a lottery, a seniority system, an optimizing formula, test scores, or arbitration.

Figure 5. Decision Process Characteristics

DECISION-MAKER RELATIONSHIPS	INTERPERSONAL DYNAMICS	PRE-DECISION POSSIBILITIES	POST-DECISION POSSIBILITIES
HIERARCHICAL	One individual exercises sole judgment	• Consult with others • Collect data • Develop perspectives • Hear adversarial debate	• Marshal support for decision implementation • Appeal the decision to a higher authority
COLLEGIAL	Synthesis of two or more points of view	• Provide training in interpersonal communication	• Follow up minority views not reflected in the group decision
ADVERSARIAL	An offer is accepted through mutual adjustment or compromise	• Form coalitions • Provide training in negotiation skills	• Ratify terms of agreement
DEMOCRATIC	Group participants accept an outside criterion	Necessary activities are: • Decide which outside criterion or rule to apply • Decide which decision options to consider	• Verify the outcome (e.g., recount the votes)

STEP 5: SELECT A DECISION PROCESS (Continued)

FOUR SITUATIONS

Situation #1: PERSONNEL ASSIGNMENTS

You are the general manager of Metropolitan Transit Authority. The Authority, a non-union organization, uses buses that are relatively old, not air-conditioned, and rather uncomfortable. However, renewed interest in mass transportation has resulted in a large purchase of buses. You will be able to replace half your bus fleet with air-conditioned, comfortable buses. They are scheduled to arrive within the month. You are responsible for deciding which of the authority's 150 drivers will be assigned to which type of bus. You run the risk of some drivers quitting or using negative tactics if they don't get assigned to a new bus.

What decision-making process would you use to decide which employees will drive which buses? Circle one.

> **A. Unilateral**
> **B. Collaboration**
> **C. Bargaining**
> **D. Decision Rule**

Situation #2: TOY SAFETY

You are president of a large toy company that sells Constructo, which is fully approved by government agencies as safe for children of all ages. After marketing the toy for two years and selling over one million sets, the first consumer safety problem occurs. A young child is strangled by swallowing a piece broken, perhaps by an adult, from your Constructo toy. The mass media has picked up the story and a lawsuit is being filed.

Which decision process would you use with your key executives to decide how to respond to this event? Circle one.

> **A. Unilateral**
> **B. Collaboration**
> **C. Bargaining**
> **D. Decision Rule**

Situation #3: DELEGATION

As manager of an aggressive, rapidly growing company, you want to position yourself to move up in your organization. You know that your chances of getting a promotion will be better if you prepare an understudy. You can be more effective in your present job, and you can develop talents of one of your subordinates, if you delegate an important project. However, in assigning one of your subordinates to this project, you risk alienating two other subordinates.

Which process would you use to decide which subordinate, of the three who deserve consideration, should be designated for the new responsibilities? Circle one.

A. Unilateral
B. Collaboration
C. Bargaining
D. Decision Rule

Situation #4: SYSTEM REVISIONS

You are the general manager of a medium-sized manufacturing company. You recently approved the installation of a new and very expensive computer system at your plant. You now believe that additional options could improve productivity. The computer vendor has submitted a revised price estimate for the system, including the new features you want. The revised price seems excessive to you and to your data processing consultant. You arrange for the vendor's people to meet with you and your consultant. You don't want to get stuck with the system you initially approved; you don't want to be overcharged for revising the system; and you don't want to risk litigation by canceling the order.

Knowing the maximum price increase you are willing to accept, which process would you use to reach a decision on a new price for the revised computer system? Circle one.

A. Unilateral
B. Collaboration
C. Bargaining
D. Decision Rule

STEP 5: SELECT A DECISION PROCESS (Continued)

AUTHOR RESPONSES TO FOUR SITUATIONS

Check how your decision process choices compare with the following answers—obtained from a research study with top-level executives.*

Situation #1: Personnel Assignments—**D. Decision Rule**

Situation #2: Toy Safety—**B. Collaboration**

Situation #3: Delegation—**A. Unilateral**

Situation #4: System Revisions—**C. Bargaining**

POWER/ALIGNMENT MODEL

The Power/Alignment model—presented in Figure 6—helps you choose the appropriate decision process in real situations. The model is based on two dimensions that thread through all four of the basic decision processes: *power* distribution and the *alignment* of stakeholder interests.

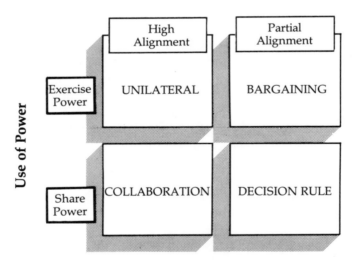

Figure 6. Power/Alignment Model: A Guide for Choosing Decision Processes

*H.S. Kindler, ''Decisions, Decisions: Which Approach to Take?'' *Personnel*, Volume 62, Number 1 (January 1985)

POWER/ALIGNMENT MODEL (Continued)

Power Distribution

A manager can either exercise power or share it. If you have the power, you can issue *unilateral* directives and have them followed. Power is also needed for *bargaining,* because each party must have the authority to make and accept offers.

Only through shared power can *collaboration* succeed in bringing together different views. When people express true feelings and real concerns, they can produce rich, mutually satisfying decisions. Power must also be shared in applying a *decision rule,* such as voting or arbitration, where the views of all participants stand a fair chance of prevailing.

Alignment of Interests

Alignment is the degree to which one party, in satisfying his or her own interests, also satisfies the interests of the other party. When two people are interdependent, such as a boss and a subordinate, some degree of alignment always exists. Such alignment may be *high*, characterized by common interests and a high level of trust, or *partial*, where some interests are mutual and some are conflicting.

ALIGN YOUR INTEREST

STEP 5: SELECT A DECISION PROCESS (Continued)

Let's look at each of the windows in Figure 6 (page 30) to see how the two dimensions, power and alignment, can help you to choose appropriate decision processes.

The Unilateral Window

When alignment is high and authority is exercised, a leader's unilateral judgment is usually accepted. For example, if a cruise ship starts to sink, the captain may bark orders directing the loading of lifeboats. Everyone knows that the captain will leave the ship last, and their needs are highly aligned because, literally, they all are in the same boat. Also, the risk of drowning is reduced because the captain is acting with the power both of position and experience.

The Collaboration Window

Peers who share a common dilemma are likely to find collaboration effective and satisfying. For example, suppose you and your partner in a tennis doubles game are equally competent, and you are losing to fairly matched opponents. You will probably want to call time out to collaborate with your partner. Working together on a joint strategy is likely to reduce your risk of defeat.

The Bargaining Window

Bargaining is a time-honored process for developing a labor-management agreement. Partial alignment exists as long as opposing sides are committed to keeping the organization viable. Both sides also must retain power, or they risk getting a less-than-favorable contract.

The Decision Rule Window

Suppose you are playing tennis again, this time in a singles match. The score is tied, and both you and your opponent have fast-approaching appointments. To end the game quickly, you might jointly accept a tie-breaking rule. In general, participants must accept decision rules *in advance* because they produce a win-lose outcome.

FOUR TEST SITUATIONS

Following is an analysis of the four test situations that demonstrate how you can apply the Power/Alignment model.

Situation #1: PERSONNEL ASSIGNMENTS

Alignment. This is a win-lose situation. If one driver is assigned a new bus, someone else loses that opportunity. Because any solution is likely to result in some discontent, these circumstances reflect partial alignment.

Power. To blunt the built-in disappointment, you should use a decision process that most drivers will see as fair. Therefore, you will want to share power with the drivers—particularly because the specific assignments will be of more concern to the individual drivers than to you.

Process. Partial alignment plus shared power = **Decision Rule.** (Note: Appropriate decision rules in this case are either a seniority system or a lottery involving driver rotation, depending on the organization's culture.)

Situation #2: TOY SAFETY

Alignment. Assuming that you and your key executives share common values related to this tragic incident, alignment among the decision makers will be high, both for personal and for organizational interests.

Power. Shared power will assure that your executives engage themselves fully in this sensitive issue, which involves difficult ethical and economic considerations.

Process. High alignment plus shared power = **Collaboration.**

STEP 5: SELECT A DECISION PROCESS (Continued)

FOUR TEST SITUATIONS (Continued)

Situation #3: DELEGATION

Alignment. If you are seen as impartial and competent in judging performance, alignment with your subordinates' need for fairness is likely to be high.

Power. Your subordinates will accept your exercise of power, provided you gather information and conduct interviews fairly, and let the candidates feel you appreciate their contributions and potential.

Process. High alignment plus exercise of power = **Unilateral Decision.**

Situation #4: SYSTEM REVISIONS

Alignment. Decision makers from each organization have partial alignment. The vendor wants to make the fewest changes and receive the maximum price; the buyer wants all the changes and a minimum price increase. Both want to maintain an ongoing relationship.

Power. Both parties need to exercise power to protect their interests while establishing a zone of agreement that offers mutual benefits.

Process. Partial alignment plus exercise of power = **Bargaining.**

Note that when you apply the Power/Alignment model to your own risky situations, you aren't simply turning a crank and getting automatic answers. You still must make subjective judgments: Is alignment high or partial? Should power be exerted or shared? You must also consider: Does confidentiality prevent the sharing of information? Does time urgency affect the choice of a decision process? However, the model does help you focus on critical considerations and avoid the pitfall of making a decision prematurely.

NOTE: The four situations that illustrate how to choose a
decision process have been adapted from the
DECISION PROCESS INVENTORY.
The complete inventory may be ordered from:
Center for Management Effectiveness
P.O. Box 1202,
Pacific Palisades,
CA 90272 • (213) 459-6052

"I'd like to place an
order for 100 copies
of DECISION PROCESS
INVENTORY please."

RECAP—SUMMARIZING TO THIS POINT:

STEP 1 **Clarify Your Goals**

Before deciding what action to take, understand *why* you are considering a risky decision.

> Suppose a friend just invested in an attractive limited partnership. You could double your money in five years if you bought in and the venture prospered. Before either leaping into or dismissing the idea out-of-hand, review your investment goals.

Examples of goals that might guide one person's investment decisions are a desire to retire in five years with a comfortable monthly income; to have funds available for special occasions and travel; and, upon her death, to help surviving family members, and also to contribute to various charities.

STEP 2 **Organize and Evaluate Alternatives**

Sort out your basic choices.

In the preceding personal investment scenario, one alternative involves putting savings at risk in a limited partnership to gain a higher return. The other choice is to invest more conservatively, perhaps in government bonds, money market funds, or insured certificates of deposit.

STEP 3 Assess Your Risk-Taking Tendencies

Understand any risk-taking inclination you may have that would bias your judgment—either toward the *excitement and adventure* of the unknown, or toward the *comfort and familiarity* of outcomes you can be reasonably sure of realizing.

STEP 4 Develop a Strategy for Change

Everything changes. The issue isn't how to maintain the status quo but how to prepare for inevitable change. You have two choices: an *incremental change strategy* (evolutionary, step-by-step), or a *transformational change strategy* (more radical, less predictable).

In the investment example, would an incremental approach, such as conservative securities, achieve your goals? If not, fundamental changes may be the only way to reach your objectives.

STEP 5 Select a Decision Process

You can either increase or reduce risk by choosing an appropriate decision process.

In personal investing, for example, a collaborative decision process with your spouse is appropriate. You share a common interest in the decision outcome and, presumably, you share power. Collaboration gives you a two-heads-are-better-than-one advantage; it provides ''training'' to the partner who may be less sophisticated in financial matters; and it precludes premature snap judgments.

You are now ready for the final planning step, and then implementation.

FIVE DOWN—THREE TO GO.

STEP 6: IMPROVE THE REWARD/RISK RATIO

To increase the odds of getting your desired outcome, and to reduce the potential for loss, consider a three-pronged approach: (A) get more information, (B) gain more control of factors that influence the outcome, and (C) reduce the impact of adverse consequences by sharing the risk.

A. Gathering Information

Gathering information can improve your decision by reducing uncertainty. Information can be collected by interviewing, direct observation, conducting surveys, and reviewing professional literature and organizational records. Before you seek additional information, weigh four factors: *time, cost, reliability*, and *relevance*.

TIME

If you take the time to gather and assimilate relevant data, will the opportunity to act be lost by the delay? Like Caesar's army poised to cross the Rubicon, is the time for a decision now or never? Determine if a delay will give competitors an irreversible advantage or otherwise hurt your position when you are ready to take action.

On the other hand, resist unnecessary or contrived deadlines requested by people who don't want you to thoroughly investigate the facts.

COST

Is the expense of acquiring more information likely to be recovered by making a better decision? This is the implicit question in poker when you risk your ante to gain information by ''buying'' more cards. Information-gathering expenses include your time and the cost of data processing, storage, and retrieval. These costs can mount until collecting data (through market research, for example) is sometimes more expensive than simply conducting the advertising campaign in question. Figure 7 shows the general relationship between the value of information and the cost of collecting it.

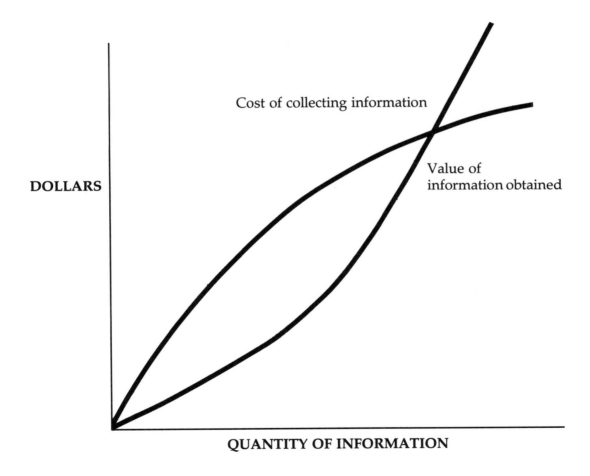

Figure 7. Evaluating the Desirability of Seeking Additional Information

STEP 6: IMPROVE THE
REWARD/RISK RATIO (Continued)

RELIABILITY

How reliable is the information you've collected? How valid and dependable are forecasts made by specialists and consultants? Whether deciding to buy gold or undergo heart surgery, have you solicited *multiple opinions?*

Is the information you obtained subject to *systematic bias?* Smoothing and censoring are common forms of bias. *Smoothing* is presenting only the good news. *Censoring* results when people with unpopular views don't want to appear out-of-step, disloyal, or negative. (Both forms of bias result when bosses are intimidating to their subordinates.)

RELEVANCE

Information is relevant when it helps answer the following questions:

- *Magnitude.* How much do you stand to lose by taking a risk?

- *Probability.* What is the likelihood you will incur a loss?

- *Exposure.* If a loss occurs, how might its impact be lessened?

B. Influencing The Outcome

If the worst-case scenario isn't acceptable, determine how you might intervene to improve the odds of realizing your goals and limiting potential losses. Explore which risk factors can be controlled in ways that are feasible, cost effective, and ethical.

Don't expect to eliminate all risk through an intervention strategy. Attempts at total control are usually self-defeating. For example, when the Hunt brothers of Dallas tried to control the price of silver by cornering bullion, they ended up losing more than $1 billion in the 1980 silver market crash. Similarly, when managers push too far to control employee behavior, subordinates become overly dependent, passive, and ultimately, resentful.

Partial control of a situation, however, is a reasonable approach to reducing risk. Consider two strategies to improve the reward/risk ratio: (1) intervene to influence critical factors; (2) develop new alternatives that transform the existing situation.

STEP 6: IMPROVE THE
REWARD/RISK RATIO (Continued)

INTERVENE

Within the bounds of ethical behavior and feasibility, you can often use your resources and influence to reduce risk.

> Suppose the enjoyment and value of your home depends on maintaining the privacy of your backyard. You want to reduce the risk that a future neighbor will build a two-story house overlooking your patio.

Your strategy could be either *proactive* or *reactive*. If you had adequate resources, you could create a buffer zone by buying the adjacent property (proactive). You could then rent, lease, or resell it to people willing to design their home in ways that assure your privacy.

Alternatively, you could take a wait-and-see stance. If your new neighbor decides to build a two-story house, you could then discuss the situation. Perhaps a clerestory or glass brick design would provide your neighbor with light and you with privacy. You might offer to contribute to extra architectural and building costs.

Seeking a court injunction (reactive) would be a last-resort strategy because, whether successful or not, it would strain future relations.

A similar range of proactive-to-reactive strategies is available in business situations. Executives, for example, may want to reduce the risk of a corporate takeover. If the company has the resources, they might choose to buy back shares of company stock. An ethical issue could arise if management buys stock from a "raider" at a premium price, which some term "greenmail." Proactive strategies include acquisitions, mergers, and alliances.

PROACTIVE STRATEGIES

Three common proactive strategies are surveillance, isolation, and buffering.

Surveillance techniques include installing plant or home security systems, screening employment applicants, and conducting unscheduled audits.

Examples of *isolation* strategies are limiting access to sensitive computer programs, locating manufacturing operations away from strong union regions, and diverting rising waters from riverside plants with dikes and sandbags.

In *buffering,* risk is reduced by maintaining a protective cushion against uncertainty. For example, bridges are designed with a cushioning "factor of safety," accidents are buffered by the use of safety shoes and glasses, inventories are stored as buffers against unanticipated demand, and spare tires are carried for emergencies.

DEVELOP NEW ALTERNATIVES

Rarely do you have to take either a conservative or a risky alternative in the form presented. You can usually invent or discover other possibilities. Consider this situation.

Paul Price is chairman and CEO of Mayco, a *Fortune 500* manufacturing corporation. Paul is highly regarded by his staff; but he feels socially isolated. He has particularly felt a lack of camaraderie during the past two years, since his wife died. About three months ago, Paul made friends at his club with Ralph Stone. They play golf almost every weekend and often enjoy dinner together.

Today, Mayco's public relations director, Jane Osgood, shocked Paul by informing him that his new friend is an ex-convict who served time for investment fraud. Continuing the friendship, she asserted, would be risky. The media might pick up the story, and negative publicity could shake investor confidence and affect the stock price. Jane urged Paul to stop seeing Ralph Stone.

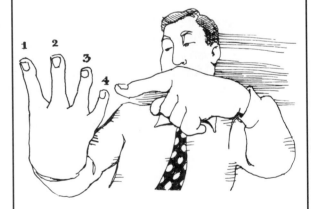

CONSIDER YOUR ALTERNATIVES

DEVELOP NEW ALTERNATIVES
(Continued)

If you were in Paul Price's shoes, you could decide to (a) continue your friendship with Ralph Stone and risk hurting innocent stockholders, or (b) give up the friendship, at least in public. What would you do?

_____

_____

_____

_____

_____

_____

_____

_____

_____

_____

_____

Particularly when neither option, risky or conservative, is attractive to you, explore new alternatives.

To start, identify and question the validity of current assumptions. In this example, the implicit assumption of the PR director is: *Ex-convicts can't be trusted.* Her conclusion: Don't associate with them.

You might challenge this assumption with a more optimistic one: *Some ex-convicts can't be trusted; others can be rehabilitated with appropriate vocational, social, and emotional support.* This reframed assumption opens possibilities of transformational change. For example, Paul Price could launch a corporate feasibility study to consider the possibility of hiring and training ex-convicts. He could appoint Ralph Stone as consultant for this project, and call a press conference to announce the study and Stone's appointment.

STEP 6: IMPROVE THE REWARD/RISK RATIO (Continued)

C. Sharing Risks

Two general strategies are available to reduce the impact of risky decisions that result in a loss: (1) Share the risk with others; (2) Limit the maximum possible loss.

SHARE THE RISK

Risk sharing can be achieved by *common ownership*. The form may be a legal entity, such as a partnership or joint venture, or a psychological bond, as gained through a collaborative decision process or joint commitment.

Another common method of distributing risk is through *insurance*. Each policy-holder pays a relatively small price so that none suffers a devastating loss. Bonding is a form of insurance for employees with access to money. In the event of theft, whether or not recovered, stolen funds are reimbursed by the insurance company.

Insurance is a feasible means of distributing risk only when the insurer can statistically predict the frequency and severity of the loss to be insured.

New ventures generally are too unpredictable for insurance underwriters. More feasible for entrepreneurs who need cash is risk-sharing with partners who provide venture capital in exchange for equity in the company. Similarly, the risk inherent in developing expensive new technology—such as low-temperature superconductors, biotechnology, and high-definition television—can be distributed via joint ventures, corporate-university consortia, and global alliances.

An increasingly important risk arena is international trade. Here, protection against sudden political and financial change is crucial. Insurance generally is available against expropriation, revolution, and insurrection. Currency swap agreements may be obtained whereby, for a fee, overseas banks guarantee the future convertibility of foreign currency at a fixed exchange rate.

Another form of risk sharing is *hedging*. When manufacturers buy futures on a commodity exchange, they reduce uncertainty. Over the long term, manufacturers of corn syrup, for example, expect to pay more for corn. By means of hedging contracts, the manufacturers can quote firm prices to customers for finished products delivered in the future. Good risk management suggests allocating some of the hedging cost to distributors and buyers, who also benefit from more stable prices.

Hedging can also be accomplished through diversification. For example, suppose you want to invest in a sun-tan lotion retail business located on a tourist island. You learn, however, that this business only flourishes during sunny days (about 75 percent of the time). On rainy days, a retail umbrella business does well. You could diversify your investment portfolio by putting 75 percent of your capital in the sun-tan business and 25 percent in the umbrella business.

LIMIT THE LOSS

Loss limiting prevents a tolerable risk from slipping into an unacceptable range. Tactics available to limit downside risk include: *stop-loss orders* to sell (anything traded in an active market) at a specific price; *safety nets,* which may break a fall or ease financial distress for a terminated executive; and *incentives* offered for the return of lost or stolen property. *Pilot-experiments* also limit losses as new products and procedures are tested in small-scale operations.

Loss limiting prevents the irrational "escalation of commitment" from occurring. Some people become so committed to a course of action, they stay with it even after it appears to be wrong. For example, people who buy stock in a company may so desperately want a profit, they refuse to sell in the face of increasing losses and projected downtrends. To walk the thin line between sticking too long with a bad decision and bailing out too soon—vigilance, stop-loss orders, and discussion with less emotionally-involved people can prove helpful.

III

Implementation

CLARIFY YOUR OBJECTIVES ❶

ORGANIZE AND EVALUATE ALTERNATIVES ❷

ASSESS YOUR RISK-TAKING TENDENCIES ❸

DEVELOP YOUR CHANGE STRATEGY ❹

SELECT A DECISION PROCESS ❺

IMPROVE REWARD-RISK RATIO ❻

OVERCOME BARRIERS ❼

ACT, EVALUATE, AND FOLLOW-UP ❽

DIAGNOSIS I

PLANNING & PREPARATION II

IMPLEMENTATION III

STEP 7: OVERCOME BARRIERS TO CONSTRUCTIVE RISK TAKING

Review the events below that led to the Challenger space shuttle tragedy.* The same issues that arose in the Challenger case also arise in everyday situations: How hard should you push a rush project? How should you handle disagreement when unforeseen circumstances develop? When should you urge your boss to reverse a directive?

Several difficulties surfaced months before the lift-off of the doomed Challenger Mission 51L. Crews were grossly overworked to maintain the NASA objective of 24 flights per year. Shuttle parts were cannibalized from one orbiter to another to hold the schedule. Missions were flying on backup systems, a violation of NASA's own long-standing rule.

Many launch crews worked 40 straight 12-hour days. One such crew inadvertently drained 18,000 pounds of liquid oxygen from the main tank of the shuttle just preceding Challenger. Had not onboard computers terminated the countdown 31 seconds before launch time, that shuttle would not have had enough fuel to reach orbit. NASA's acting administrator, William Graham, lied to the press, saying the problem was a "mechanical failure."

Safety was, and remains, NASA's central risk concern. But by the time of the Challenger launch, NASA was in the process of cutting its safety budget by half a billion dollars and its quality control staff by 70 percent.

---

*Reference sources used for the information in this case are: P. M. Boffey, "Analyst Who Gave Shuttle Warning Faults 'Gung-Ho, Can-Do' Attitude," *New York Times*, February 14, 1986; P. M. Boffey, "Shuttle Officials Deny Pressuring Rocket Engineers," *New York Times*, February 27, 1986; D. E. Sanger, "Communications Channels at NASA: Warnings That Faded Along the Line," *New York Times*, February 28, 1986; J. J. and S. B. Trento, "Why Challenger Was Doomed," *Los Angeles Times*, January 18, 1987; T. E. Bell and K. Esch, "The Fatal Flaw in Flight 51L," *IEEE Spectrum*, February 1988, 36–51.

OVERCOME BARRIERS
(Continued)

By the end of 1985, the O-ring safety seals for the shuttle's solid rocket boosters had failed on 10 out of 23 flights. Thiokol senior engineer Roger Boisjoly, a specialist in the seals, informed his management in a July 31, 1985 memo that the consequence of not solving the seal problem "would be a catastrophe of the highest order—loss of human life." Within NASA, budget analyst Richard Cook warned agency executives, in his July 23, 1985 memo, that flight safety was "being compromised by potential erosion of the seals" and that a catastrophe might result. NASA officials later said they had discounted Cook's warnings as overstating the concerns of propulsion engineers because he was "new and inexperienced."

The following events took place the evening before Challenger was scheduled to be launched, after four postponements.

January 27, 1986 2:30 p.m. Because an overnight low of 18°F (−8°C) was forecast for the Kennedy Space Center, NASA asked Thiokol to review the cold snap's possible effects. The engineering conclusion: subfreezing temperatures could dangerously stiffen the already problematic synthetic rubber O-ring seals.

8:45 p.m. A teleconference began among 34 NASA and Thiokol engineers and managers. After a technical discussion, Thiokol's vice president said he could not recommend a launch at temperatures below 53°F (25°C), the limit of their experience. A NASA executive remarked, "My God, Thiokol, when do you want me to fly? Next April?"

Thiokol interrupted the phone discussion for a private caucus. The managers agreed to override the unanimous objections of their engineers and decided to risk a launch in cold weather.

The Rogers Commission, created by President Ronald Reagan, concluded that the death of Challenger's seven astronauts and passengers was caused by failure of the space vehicle's booster O-rings. They further asserted, "The fundamental problem was poor decision making over a period of several years by top NASA and contractor personnel."

Several barriers impeded the use of an effective decision-making process in the Challenger case. These barriers were also present in other historical situations.

Risk Taking

STEP 7: OVERCOME BARRIERS (Continued)

OTHER EXAMPLES

"How could we have been so stupid?" President John F. Kennedy asked after he and a group of close advisors launched the ill-fated Bay of Pigs invasion in Cuba. Why did such bright men uncritically accept the Central Intelligence Agency's disastrous plan? Why was the U.S. military command in Hawaii unprepared for the possibility of a Japanese attack in 1941 on Pearl Harbor *despite repeated warnings?* Why did President Lyndon Johnson and his "in-group" advisors keep escalating the Vietnam War despite repeated setbacks and failures? President Nixon and his staff continued to cover up the notorious Watergate burglary of Democratic election headquarters despite evidence of adverse consequences. One White House assistant explained to U.S. Senators that he feared the group would label him as not being a team player, and he wanted to be seen as a loyal member of the President's staff.

In studying these blunders, Irving Janis found a common thread that he termed "groupthink."* The term is used to describe the social pressure that close-knit groups generate that tends to short-circuit consideration of alternatives.

Hidden from news media, but even more common than public debacles, the same barriers to sound risk taking occur daily in organizational life. Managers can learn crucial lessons from the Challenger disaster. When working with others in risky situations, you will meet three common barriers.

---

*I. L. Janis, *Victims of Groupthink,* Boston: Houghton Mifflin, 1972.

BARRIER 1 | **Ignoring the moral consequences of your decision**

OVERCOME BY | **Clarifying stakeholder values**

Deciding whether a risk is acceptable requires judging *probability* and *severity* of the possible loss. Probability often can be determined by statistical methods; but judging severity depends on the *subjective valuing* of stakeholders—people who have a stake in the outcome. ''Valuing'' means balancing the most desired against the least desired consequences of taking the risk.

Valuing depends on individual perceptions of clearly understood conditions at a given point in time. For example, a skier knowing snow conditions and hazards may choose to risk skiing a particular slope. At a later stage in life, the same person may choose not to head down the identical slope because of greater physical fragility or increased family responsibilities. The only way to know how stakeholders value a specific risk is to provide clear, accurate information and then *ask them.*

Even when stakeholders are well informed, another problem associated with values may surface. To appreciate this problem, please rank the following four values: money, love, family, status. In the box below, write the value you most desire on line 1, your second preference on line 2 and so on.

MONEY	LOVE	FAMILY	STATUS
1. _____			
2. _____			
3. _____			
4. _____			

STEP 7: OVERCOME BARRIERS (Continued)

OVERCOMING BARRIER 1 (Continued)

Now, assume you are the executive in the following scenario.

> Three years ago, you and your family moved to a new city so you could accept your current job assignment. Your spouse thoroughly enjoys this community and your present lifestyle; your two children have made friends and like their school. Unexpectedly, you are offered the career opportunity of a lifetime—a promotion that places you in charge of an entire division of some 3,000 employees and an incredible raise with attractive perquisites. However, to accept this opportunity, you need to relocate again. If you turn down the offer, future advancement with this organization is unlikely. You feel qualified for the promotion and, if you accept, you are likely to succeed in the new position.

What is your reaction to the offer of promotion?

Accept _____ **Decline** _____

In an earlier exercise, almost all middle managers (in a sample of 150 men and 50 women surveyed by the author) ranked love and family higher than money and status. Yet, in responding to the scenario, a majority (with a much higher percentage of men than women) decided to disrupt their family life when given a one-time opportunity for money and status. A common justification was: ''In the long run, my family's benefits will be greater if we make one more move to another city.'' Others said that—like an overweight dieter who is offered a hot-fudge sundae—the opportunity was just too tempting to resist.

In the Challenger case, the highest value of NASA executives, according to their publicity releases, was human safety. Yet their behavior appears to have been motivated by values other than safety. For example, of the four contractor companies that submitted proposals to NASA, Thiokol's engineering design was evaluated *lowest* in terms of soundness. Thiokol was selected for economic, not human values—its bid was $100 million under the next lowest competitor. To reduce costs further, deep cuts were made in the number of NASA inspectors overseeing contractors' work. Reductions in the safety and quality assurance staff were deep compared with other personnel cuts. Finally, the decision to launch at untested, subfreezing temperatures is not consistent with a primary concern for human safety.

Imagine if the seven people who were to be orbited into space had been informed or consulted about launching in cold weather—Thiokol's engineers would have been listened to by the astronauts whose lives depended on NASA taking reasonable risks.

Where values are a key factor in a risky situation, it is vital to involve stakeholders in talking about how well a course of action fits those values. Open discussion, including expression of feelings, helps get to the heart of the principles and standards that really matter.

STEP 7: OVERCOME BARRIERS (Continued)

| BARRIER 2 | Feeling pressured

| OVERCOME BY | Reframing, releasing, and recruiting support

Risky situations generate two types of pressure: external and self-generated.

External pressure is easier to identify than the demands we place on ourselves. It takes such form as: an unreasonable schedule, group expectations, an aggressive competitor or rival, personal problems at home. External pressure can cloud perception, particularly when it is unexpected, beyond your control, or the stakes are high.

In the Challenger case, the decision makers faced multiple pressures. NASA Administrator James Beggs was convinced that a dramatically successful shuttle would build congressional and public support for his vision of a space station. He personally spoke to the President, and $150 million was added to the 1985 budget for preliminary planning of a space station. Beggs pressured his managers to accelerate and vastly expand the shuttle's schedule. His managers, in turn, pressured contractors. For example, in the teleconference between NASA and Thiokol, on the eve of the scheduled Challenger launch, a NASA manager said that while he would not proceed against Thiokol's recommendation, he was "appalled" that Thiokol would recommend a delay in launching. Thiokol quickly reversed its recommendation.

More pervasive and subtle than external pressure is each person's internalized "pusher" and "critic." Self-generated pressure is expressed as anxiety and fear, producing such behaviors as perfectionism, procrastination, and dysfunctional decision making.

External and internal pressures usually act in tandem. For example:

> Suppose two people have lost their savings in a poor investment. Person A perceives his financial loss as devastating and sees himself as a victim of circumstance. Person B sees her misfortune as a temporary setback and defines her situation in terms of a solvable cash-flow problem.

Distressed person A is less likely than person B to take future risks in a balanced or flexible manner. Research shows that people who have a *strong need to avoid failure* become either ultra-cautious or rash in their risk-taking behavior.* In the above example, person A may feel so anxious about risk taking that he tries to avoid any possibility of future loss. Alternatively, he may feel so hopeless that he will attempt to recoup his financial losses and soothe his injured pride by taking risks recklessly.

To protect yourself from being pressured into inappropriate decisions:

1. *Reframe the situation to reduce the pressure.*
   Reframing means changing the conceptual setting or emotional orientation of the situation, to allow a new interpretation of the same "facts." Reframing shifts perception to create a new perspective.

   For example, suppose your boss promotes a colleague to a position you expected to get. You could feel crushed and decide your boss doesn't like you. Or you could reframe the situation as an opportunity to let your boss know about your career aspirations and to ask how you might prepare for the next opportunity.

---

*J. W. Atkinson, "Motivational Determinants of Risk-Taking Behavior," *Psychological Review*, 1957, pp. 359–372.

STEP 7: OVERCOME BARRIERS (Continued)

OVERCOMING BARRIER 2   (Continued)

Another approach to reframing is to ask what lessons you might learn about yourself when you feel pressured.

In the example—where your boss promoted another person to the position you expected—you could review such self-learning questions as: How come your colleague's promotion was a surprise to you? How might you be more sensitive to future signals? Was your colleague better qualified or simply better appreciated? Do you have adequate rapport with your boss?

2. *Release anger and resentment.*
   When we lose a well-deserved promotion or feel betrayed, anger and resentment are normal reactions. However, deciding on your next step—reframing, confronting, departing, or initiating an appeal procedure—requires a cool head.

   Find a way to release anger that works for you and doesn't hurt anyone else. Some people pound their frustration into a track or punching bag; others yell with their car windows rolled up; still others write nasty letters and burn them unmailed. The ultimate release for resentment is forgiveness. No matter how justified our anger, we carry it at a high cost to ourselves—it clouds our judgment and undermines our health.*

3. *Muster outside support.*
   Your friends, family, and compassionate co-workers are a resource for reducing excessive pressure. These people—your social network—may be able to provide encouragement, humor, and a fresh perspective.

   For example, if you decide to risk confronting your boss to explore future job opportunities and options, you could rehearse the discussion with a friend first to get helpful feedback.

---

*For a thorough discussion of releasing negative emotions and expectations, see Chapter 13, ''Letting Go,'' in H. S. Kindler and M. Ginsburg, *Stress Training For Life*, New York: Nichols Publishing, 1990.

BARRIER 3 | Failing to tap available information

OVERCOME BY | Helping people express dissident views

When vital information is withheld or distorted, decision makers neglect valid alternatives, act prematurely, and take unwarranted risks. Therefore, leaders must solicit views that challenge dominant attitudes and assumptions.

In the Challenger case, the dominant NASA attitude—based on a history of success—was ''can't fail'' complacency. Anyone with the courage to point out a possible weakness was discredited, discounted, or ostracized. When a NASA analyst waved a red flag about the O-ring seals, he was labelled ''too new and inexperienced.'' In return for his candor at the government hearings, engineer Boisjoly was treated at work like a social outcast. A Rockwell vice president testified that he explicitly told NASA officials, ''Rockwell cannot assure that it is safe to fly in the prevailing ice conditions.'' NASA managers skewed their interpretation of this statement to mean a cautious recommendation in favor of launching.

''THESE NICE FOLKS HAVE AGREED
TO GIVE US THEIR VIEWS''

STEP 7: OVERCOME BARRIERS (Continued)

OVERCOMING BARRIER 3   (Continued)

To get the lifeblood of appropriate risk taking pumped into your decision process, you need relevant, accurate, timely information. Build bridges that invite the expression of divergent views as follows:.

1. *Don't express your preference too quickly.*
   During the Kennedy administration's Cuban missile crisis, the President avoided influencing his advisors by not even attending their initial meetings.* The group's quick consensus was to bomb Cuban missile silos before the Russian-made weapons became operational, which would be in a matter of days. However, only after several other possibilities were discussed—a summit conference, secret negotiations, a naval blockade—did the blockade become the group's recommended plan.

   To avoid premature convergence on a course of action, Alfred Sloan, former chairman of General Motors, delayed decisions whenever a group started with complete agreement. He would propose that action be deferred until there was enough disagreement to give insight into the underlying issues. Other leaders develop opposing views and counterplans to spark creative ideas—this is the approach of the British House of Commons, with its traditional "loyal opposition."

---

*Information about the Cuban missile crisis is based on Graham Allison's *Essence of Decision: Explaining the Cuban Missile Crisis*, Boston: Little, Brown, 1971.

2. *Encourage critical feedback.*

People express critical thoughts and negative feelings reluctantly, if at all. At workshops conducted by the author, the reasons most frequently given for not telling co-workers about annoying behaviors are:

- I don't want to hurt the other person's feelings.
- I'm not sure how others will react; they may get angry.
- I don't want to start an argument.
- The other person will either deny what I say or shift the blame.
- I'm not interested in getting others stirred up, especially when I have to work with these people every day.

The consequences of employees' reluctance to be candid with one another is illustrated by the story of Carl.

> Carl, a near-genius, doesn't listen well and dominates every meeting he attends. Early in his career, no one wanted to hurt Carl's feelings by telling him that his insensitivity was irritating. After Carl moved up the organization ladder, he became even less accessible to critical feedback. When Carl's vice president retired, Carl applied for the position. He was turned down.

Ironically, because Carl's associates didn't want to hurt his feelings, he never got the feedback that would have enabled him to succeed when he applied for a really significant promotion.

STEP 7: OVERCOME BARRIERS (Continued)

| OVERCOMING BARRIER 3 | (Continued)

To get needed feedback, consider these approaches:

- *Invite critical perspectives* of people whose views you value. Don't cut off vital feedback by requiring a solution from someone who may not be able to provide one.

- *Provide a context* that allows the other person to understand your intent. Say *why* you want feedback. Do you want to discuss a performance concern? Do you want to develop a more satisfying relationship?

- *Ask if your behavior is a problem for the other person.* The real challenge for managers is not how to motivate employees, but how to *remove obstacles* that impede their productivity.

3. *Encourage communication from subordinates.*
   The central problem of upward communication is that employees tend to send up only those messages that put them in a favorable light. To encourage the flow of accurate information to decision makers:

- *Develop an open-minded culture.* An open-door policy is more fiction than fact in most companies. At IBM, however, if subordinates can't reach agreement with a boss, each boss arranges for the subordinate to discuss the issue at successively higher levels. Ultimately, some employee concerns reach the CEO. When Tom Watson, Jr., was in that position at IBM, he was asked how he could afford to take the time to review issues brought through the chain of command. His succinct answer: ''How can I afford not to!''

- *Consult people outside the regular chain of command.* Following the Challenger tragedy, NASA created the new position of ombudsman, appointing a senior executive accessible to all employees. The NASA ombudsman was given authority to stop a shuttle launching; other organizations limit the ombudsman's domain to communication and problem-solving mediation. These executives are available to everyone in the hierarchy to help identify concerns important to risk-taking decisions.

  Other potential sources of valuable information are key customers, suppliers, contractors, and community representatives.

- *Provide training in interpersonal communication skills.* Start skill-building training—especially the management of interpersonal differences—with top executives. In this way, you make it a low-risk program for others to take. By offering formal workshops on managing disagreement, the organization demonstrates its support for the expression of dissident views.*

STEP 8

---

*For a workbook that supports this type of training, order MANAGING DISAGREEMENT CONSTRUCTIVELY using the form in the back of this book.

STEP 8: ACT, EVALUATE, AND FOLLOW-UP

A. Take Action

Your decision may be implemented easily or with difficulty. Deciding how to invest one's life savings may be tough, but once the decision is made, checks can easily be written and mailed.

Implementing your decision to market a new product, on the other hand, is an arduous venture requiring continuing attention—and further risk taking. For complex activities, develop a *written implementation plan,* with input from the people you depend on to make it work. Your action plan may include cash-flow projections, critical events requiring tight coordination, and the assignment of responsibilities. Additionally, for situations with high levels of uncertainty, include a *contingency plan* with criteria for triggering it.

Before committing full resources, determine if a small-scale operation or trial run are feasible and meaningful options.

Most people have experienced "buyer's remorse" or felt some postdecision regret. Acknowledge these feelings, but don't let anxiety make you compulsively cautious.

B. Evaluate Progress

Establish criteria by which to judge whether your implementation effort is getting desired results. In some cases, you will have established these criteria already in reaching your decision. For example, in the 1962 Cuban missile crisis, criteria presented in Figure 8 (facing page) would likely have been developed before President Kennedy's naval blockade decision was made. Figure 8 illustrates a simple quantitative approach to evaluating success based both on facts and subjective judgment.

EVALUATION OF THE CUBAN MISSILE CRISIS DECISION

EXPECTED OUTCOME	RATING BASED ON EXPECTED OUTCOME	RATING BASED ON ACTUAL OUTCOME
		(Scale: 1 to 10)
1. Missiles will be removed within one month.	6	_____
2. World opinion will remain favorably disposed to the U.S.	8	_____
3. United States public will support President Kennedy's position.	9	_____
4. Sino-Soviet relations will not be strengthened.	8	_____
5. United States–Soviet disarmament talks will remain a possibility.	6	_____
TOTALS	37	_____

Figure 8. Criteria for Evaluating Implementation Results

The same people who agreed to the initial ratings (in this case, Kennedy and his advisors) should review the consequences of implementing the decision. The evaluation should be conducted at a pre-established date when a midcourse correction still can be made.

One caution about group evaluation: Be wary of strong *advocates*, people who were passionate about the specific final decision. They may interpret events in ways that support their choice, overlooking potential trouble signs. Similarly, those who were unconvinced about the final decision or felt it was forced on them, may misinterpret favorable signs.

STEP 8: ACT, EVALUATE AND FOLLOW-UP (Continued)

C. Follow Up

If outcomes don't satisfy your expectations, and if a correction is feasible, a modest *incremental change* may suffice. Alternatively, remain open to the possibility of a radical *transformational change*—undoing the original decision and moving in another direction.

If a major change is called for, decision makers may be reluctant to write off sunk costs. Sunk cost has no economic value (by definition, sunk cost cannot be recovered), but it can be a psychological barrier to change. Decision makers may become overcommitted to implementing a bad decision (like beating the proverbial dead horse) to protect their pride or reputation. If you suspect this excessive attachment to the original plan, a less involved person may provide more objectivity.

Finally, take the time to ask yourself what you might do differently to be more effective in future risky situations. Risk, at its core, is a measure of ignorance. Our challenge is to illuminate those dark places where we are excessively vulnerable. Conscious risk taking—assessing risk with care and managing it prudently—underpins all professional and personal growth.

Summary Review

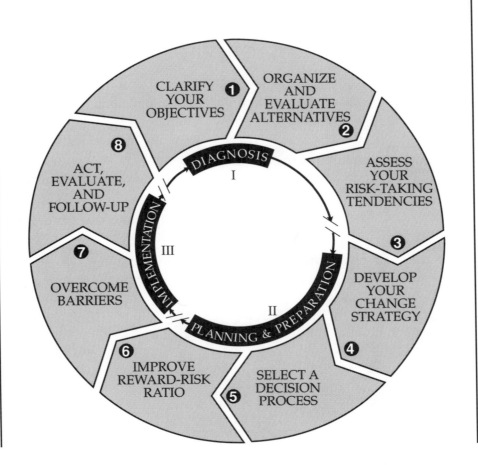

SUMMARY REVIEW

PART I. Diagnosis

| Step 1 | *Clarify the objectives that risk taking may advance.*
Before deciding on a course of action, sharpen your focus on why the action is important to take. Is the potential loss worth the desired gain?

| Step 2 | *Organize and evaluate the basic alternatives.*
Develop a format that allows you to compare the merits of each option.

| Step 3 | *Assess your risk-taking tendencies.*
Understand any bias you may have either toward seeking risk or avoiding it.

PART II. Planning and Preparation

| Step 4 | *Develop a strategy for change.*
Consider two basic strategies: incremental (branch) and transformational (root) change.

| Step 5 | *Select a decision process.*
Consider four decision processes: unilateral, collaboration, bargaining, and decision rule.

| Step 6 | *Increase the reward/risk ratio.*
To improve the odds of realizing your risk-taking goals and to reduce the chances of suffering a loss:

A. Gather information (considering the demands of time and cost and the need for reliability and relevance).

B. Gain more control over the outcome.

C. Reduce your exposure to loss by risk-sharing and loss-limiting tactics.

PART III. Implementation

| Step 7 | *Overcome the barriers to constructive risk taking.*
Consider the moral consequences of your decision. Reduce the pressure of both external and self-generated sources. Encourage the expression of divergent views.

| Step 8 | *Take action, evaluate outcome and follow-up.*
Develop your implementation plan, check your post-decision reactions, evaluate progress, make required midcourse corrections, monitor the decision outcome over time, and learn from your experience.

Good luck!

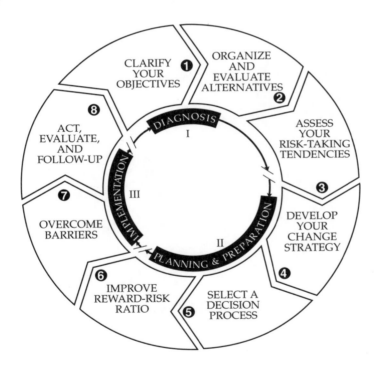

RISK-TAKING ASSESSMENT GUIDE

Making Choices under Conditions of Uncertainty

This Guide enables you to apply the complete risk-taking framework presented in this book to personal, career, and organizational issues.

We have provided a completed guide to show you how it's done. This is followed by a blank inventory for your use.

Individual copies of the Risk-Taking Assessment Guide are available in booklet form from the Center for Management Effectiveness, P.O. Box 1202, Pacific Palisades, CA 90272. (213) 459-6052

RISK-TAKING ASSESSMENT GUIDE

1. Briefly describe a *problem situation* involving risk that concerns you.

My job lacks challenge, excitement, and the opportunity
to earn a lot more money. It provides me with steady
income, my performance is recognized, and my
pay is fair. I feel a pull to become an independent
consultant. If I don't act during the coming 2-3 years,
before we start our family, I may never take
the risk.

2. With respect to this situation, indicate your *principal objective*, what really matters.

I want to feel good about going to work each day
because it is stimulating, pays well, and provides
opportunities for me to learn and improve my skills.

© 1989 H. S. Kindler, Ph.D.

POTENTIAL OPTIONS

3. Identify *options* that could lead to your objective or help resolve your problem. Also, reframe the problem in ways that open new alternatives with fresh possibilities.

(a) *I could keep my present position, and find ways to continually enrich and upgrade it over time, or get promoted.*

(b) *I could find a more challenging job elsewhere in a related field.*

(c) *I could start my own business as a consultant, building on my experience and expertise.*

(d) _____

RISK-TAKING ASSESSMENT GUIDE
(Continued)

4. List key *stakeholders* in this situation; that is, people who will be significantly affected by the decision. Also, specify which decision processes are most appropriate for each stakeholder.

STAKEHOLDERS	DECISION PROCESS

(a) _My wife and I_
(we really should be deciding this issue together)

☐ Unilateral
☑ Collaboration
☐ Bargaining
☐ Decision Rule

(b) _My current boss and I_

☐ Unilateral
☑ Collaboration
☑ Bargaining
☐ Decision Rule

(c) _Potential clients (for whom I would consult)_

☐ Unilateral
☑ Collaboration
☐ Bargaining
☐ Decision Rule

(d) _Potential employers_

☐ Unilateral
☑ Collaboration
☑ Bargaining
☐ Decision Rule

(e) _____

☐ Unilateral
☐ Collaboration
☐ Bargaining
☐ Decision Rule

(f) _____

☐ Unilateral
☐ Collaboration
☐ Bargaining
☐ Decision Rule

RESERVATIONS AND RISKS FOR EACH CHANGE OPTION

5. For each option you identified, indicate with a check-mark which *type of change* is appropriate. ("Incremental" is a step-by-step change; "transformational" is a more radical change.) Also, list your concerns and any additional information you want to gather.

OPTION

(a) *Enrich or upgrade my present position*

TYPE OF CHANGE

☑ Incremental

☐ Transformational

Indicate your concerns and missing information.

I'm not sure I can go any further with my current employer, or that I would be given the opportunity to assume greater responsibility. I want to check this out. If advancement or job enrichment are real possibilities, how soon?

OPTION

(b) *Find a more challenging salaried job with another employer.*

TYPE OF CHANGE

☑ Incremental

☐ Transformational

Indicate your concerns and missing information.

I have 15 years seniority and fringe benefits that I prefer not to lose. I would like to know what other jobs may be available, as well as compensation and career advancement opportunities.

RISK-TAKING ASSESSMENT GUIDE
(Continued)

OPTION

(c) _Start my own consulting_
business.

TYPE OF CHANGE

☐ Incremental

☑ Transformational

Indicate your concerns and missing information.

I feel anxious about making monthly mortgage
payments without any predictable monthly
income. I want to find out if I can line up one
or two substantial clients before giving up my
job.

OPTION

(d) _____

TYPE OF CHANGE

☐ Incremental

☐ Transformational

Indicate your concerns and missing information.

REWARD/RISK IMPROVEMENT

6. *Risk adjustment.* For each option, indicate how you will improve your reward/risk ratio. Consider alliances, collaboration, insurance, hedges, buffers, and safety nets.

OPTION

(a) _Enrich or upgrade my present position._

Indicate how you will obtain desired information, influence preferred outcomes, limit potential loss, and share risks.

Discuss opportunities with my boss for added responsibilities and future career advancement. Connect with a mentor in the company who knows the ropes.

OPTION

(b) _Find a better job elsewhere_

Indicate how you will obtain desired information, influence preferred outcomes, limit potential loss, and share risks.

Network with acquaintances at other companies. Get more involved in my professional association's activities.

RISK-TAKING ASSESSMENT GUIDE
(Continued)

OPTION

(c) _Start my own consulting business_

Indicate how you will obtain desired information, influence preferred outcomes, limit potential loss, and share risks.

I may be able to interest a friend in forming a consulting partnership. I could get a part-time job to assure steady income as the business builds momentum. My wife and I could reduce personal expenses. I could enroll in an MBA program to improve my odds of managing a successful venture.

OPTION

(d) _Earn an MBA degree, then start my consulting practice_

Indicate how you will obtain desired information, influence preferred outcomes, limit potential loss, and share risks.

I'll check with State University to learn the cost, time and energy required to get a master's degree in business administration. It would help attract clients and expand my support network.

DECISION ASSESSMENT MATRIX INSTRUCTIONS

The matrix on page 78 brings your preferred course of action into focus. Complete it after you have gathered important missing information.

Instructions for completing Decision Assessment Matrix

1. Under DESIRED OUTCOME, write a brief phrase that identifies each benefit you hope to realize in resolving your problem situation. (If you have more than four hoped-for outcomes, draw a larger matrix.)

2. Under OPTION, write a brief phrase that identifies each course of action you are considering. (If you have more than four options under consideration draw a larger matrix.)

3. Decide how much you value DESIRED OUTCOME (1) on a scale from 1 to 10, where 10 is highest. Write your score under ''Outcome Value'' for *all* Options.

4. Decide how much you value DESIRED OUTCOME (2) on a scale from 1 to 10. Write your score under ''Outcome Value'' for *all* Options. Repeat this process for DESIRED OUTCOME (3) and (4).

5. Starting with OPTION (a), decide the *probability* that it would produce DESIRED OUTCOME (1). Write your rating, from 1 to 10, under ''Option Probability Rating'' for OPTION (a). Repeat this process for OPTION (b), (c), and (d).

6. Return to OPTION (a) and evaluate the probability that it would produce DESIRED OUTCOME (2). Write your rating for OPTION (a). Repeat this process for OPTION (b), (c), and (d).

7. Repeat Step 6 for OUTCOME (3) and (4).

8. For OPTION (a) multiply each ''Outcome Value'' by its ''Option Probability Rating'' and add the results. Repeat this process for OPTIONS (b), (c), and (d).

Note: This procedure may appear complex. Using the matrix is really simple, as illustrated by the completed form.

DECISION ASSESSMENT MATRIX

DESIRED OUTCOME	OPTION							
	(a) Enrich current position		(b) Find new job		(c) Start own business with partner		(d) Get MBA, then start business	
	Outcome Value ×	Option Probability Rating	Outcome Value ×	Option Probability Rating	Outcome Value ×	Option Probability Rating	Outcome Value ×	Option Probability Rating
(1) Stimulating work	$10 \times 4 =$	40	$10 \times 7 =$	70	$10 \times 9 =$	90	$10 \times 10 =$	100
(2) Dependable income	$9 \times 10 =$	90	$9 \times 8 =$	72	$9 \times 2 =$	18	$9 \times 6 =$	54
(3) Potential to substantially increase income	$8 \times 2 =$	16	$8 \times 3 =$	24	$8 \times 8 =$	64	$8 \times 9 =$	72
(4) More autonomy	$7 \times 5 =$	35	$7 \times 6 =$	42	$7 \times 10 =$	70	$7 \times 10 =$	70
TOTAL		181		208		242		296

YOUR DECISION

Generally, your best option will:

- Score 15 percent higher than the closest alternative.
- Have a high probability of producing your most desired outcomes.
- Fall within your comfort zone.

If two or more options have close scores or if you have a negative ''gut feeling,'' check these questions:

- Did you state your desired outcomes fully, or do you have important hoped-for outcomes to add?
- Do your assigned values reasonably reflect your priorities?
- Have you overlooked options that deserve consideration?
- Do you need to collect more information?
- Can you combine features of two or more options to develop a superior course of action?

Retain this completed *Risk Taking Assessment Guide*. It will help you evaluate actual outcomes after you implement your decision.

RISK-TAKING ASSESSMENT GUIDE (Continued)

1. Briefly describe a *problem situation* involving risk that concerns you.

_____

_____

_____

_____

_____

_____

_____

2. With respect to this situation, indicate your *principal objective*, what really matters.

_____

_____

_____

_____

_____

_____

_____

POTENTIAL OPTIONS

3. Identify *options* that could lead to your objective or help resolve your problem. Also, reframe the problem in ways that open new alternatives with fresh possibilities.

(a) _____

_____

_____

_____

(b) _____

_____

_____

_____

(c) _____

_____

_____

_____

_____

(d) _____

_____

_____

_____

RISK-TAKING ASSESSMENT GUIDE
(Continued)

4. List key *stakeholders* in this situation; that is, people who will be significantly affected by the decision. Also, specify which decision processes are most appropriate for each stakeholder.

STAKEHOLDERS	DECISION PROCESS

(a) _____
- ☐ Unilateral
- ☐ Collaboration
- ☐ Bargaining
- ☐ Decision Rule

(b) _____
- ☐ Unilateral
- ☐ Collaboration
- ☐ Bargaining
- ☐ Decision Rule

(c) _____
- ☐ Unilateral
- ☐ Collaboration
- ☐ Bargaining
- ☐ Decision Rule

(d) _____
- ☐ Unilateral
- ☐ Collaboration
- ☐ Bargaining
- ☐ Decision Rule

(e) _____
- ☐ Unilateral
- ☐ Collaboration
- ☐ Bargaining
- ☐ Decision Rule

(f) _____
- ☐ Unilateral
- ☐ Collaboration
- ☐ Bargaining
- ☐ Decision Rule

RESERVATIONS AND RISKS FOR EACH CHANGE OPTION

5. For each option you identified, indicate with a check-mark which *type of change* is appropriate. (''Incremental'' is a step-by-step change; ''transformational'' is a more radical change.) Also, list your concerns and any additional information you want to gather.

OPTION   **TYPE OF CHANGE**

(a) _____   ☐ Incremental

_____   ☐ Transformational

Indicate your concerns and missing information.

_____

_____

_____

_____

_____

_____

OPTION   **TYPE OF CHANGE**

(b) _____   ☐ Incremental

_____   ☐ Transformational

Indicate your concerns and missing information.

_____

_____

_____

_____

_____

RISK-TAKING ASSESSMENT GUIDE
(Continued)

OPTION   **TYPE OF CHANGE**

(c) _____   ☐ Incremental

_____   ☐ Transformational

_____

Indicate your concerns and missing information.

_____

_____

_____

_____

_____

_____

OPTION   **TYPE OF CHANGE**

(d) _____   ☐ Incremental

_____   ☐ Transformational

_____

Indicate your concerns and missing information.

_____

_____

_____

_____

_____

REWARD/RISK IMPROVEMENT

6. *Risk adjustment.* For each option, indicate how you will improve your reward/risk ratio. Consider alliances, collaboration, insurance, hedges, buffers, and safety nets.

OPTION

(a) _____

_____

_____

Indicate how you will obtain desired information, influence preferred outcomes, limit potential loss, and share risks.

_____

_____

_____

_____

_____

OPTION

(b) _____

_____

_____

Indicate how you will obtain desired information, influence preferred outcomes, limit potential loss, and share risks.

_____

_____

_____

_____

_____

RISK-TAKING ASSESSMENT GUIDE
(Continued)

OPTION

(c) _____

_____

_____

Indicate how you will obtain desired information, influence preferred outcomes, limit potential loss, and share risks.

_____

_____

_____

_____

_____

OPTION

(d) _____

_____

_____

Indicate how you will obtain desired information, influence preferred outcomes, limit potential loss, and share risks.

_____

_____

_____

_____

_____

DECISION ASSESSMENT MATRIX

	OPTION			
	(a)	(b)	(c)	(d)
DESIRED OUTCOME	Outcome Value × Option Probability Rating	Outcome Value × Option Probability Rating	Outcome Value × Option Probability Rating	Outcome Value × Option Probability Rating
(1)	× =	× =	× =	× =
(2)	× =	× =	× =	× =
(3)	× =	× =	× =	× =
(4)	× =	× =	× =	× =
TOTAL				

Note: See pages 76-77 for instructions on how to complete the Decision Assessment Matrix.

OTHER SOURCES

This book offers concise, practical coverage of risk taking for decision makers. The following books are more theoretical. Following each reference, the book's general orientation is indicated.

Bernard M. Bass, *Organizational Decision Making*, Homewood, Illinois: Irwin, 1983, 223 pages. Both a scholarly and practical book about the decision process as applied to business policy, strategic planning, and organization design.

Irving L. Janis and Leon Mann, *Decision Making: A Psychological Analysis of Conflict, Choice, and Commitment*, New York: Free Press, 1977, 488 pages. Provides a coherent theory of how people cope with decision conflict in both personal and organizational situations.

Kenneth R. MacCrimmon and Donald A. Wehrung, *Taking Risks: The Management of Uncertainty*, New York: Free Press, 1986, 380 pages. This book is the most comprehensive work to date on research studies of managerial risk taking.

Paul C. Nutt, *Making Tough Decisions*, San Francisco: Jossey-Bass, 1989, 609 pages. Integrates information about managerial decision making from social psychology, organization theory, decision analysis, and systems theory.

Ellen Y. Siegelman, *Personal Risk: Mastering Change in Love and Work*, New York: Harper & Row, 1983, 157 pages. This highly readable book focuses on making major life changes, largely from a psychological perspective.

W.T. Singleton and J. Hoyden, Editors, *Risk and Decision*, New York: Wiley, 1987, 232 pages. This collection of research-oriented seminar papers focuses on occupational health and safety.

NOTES

NOTES

FOR OTHER FIFTY-MINUTE SELF-STUDY BOOKS
SEE ORDER FORM AT THE BACK OF THE BOOK.

NOTES

NOTES

FOR OTHER FIFTY-MINUTE SELF-STUDY BOOKS
SEE ORDER FORM AT THE BACK OF THE BOOK.

NOTES

NOTES

THE FIFTY-MINUTE SERIES

Quantity	Title	Code #	Price	Amount
	MANAGEMENT TRAINING			
	Self-Managing Teams	000-0	$7.95	
	Delegating For Results	008-6	$7.95	
	Successful Negotiation—Revised	09-2	$7.95	
	Increasing Employee Productivity	010-8	$7.95	
	Personal Performance Contracts—Revised	12-2	$7.95	
	Team Building—Revised	16-5	$7.95	
	Effective Meeting Skills	33-5	$7.95	
	An Honest Day's Work: Motivating Employees To Excel	39-4	$7.95	
	Managing Disagreement Constructively	41-6	$7.95	
	Training Managers To Train	43-2	$7.95	
	Learning To Lead	043-4	$7.95	
	The Fifty-Minute Supervisor—Revised	58-0	$7.95	
	Leadership Skills For Women	62-9	$7.95	
	Systematic Problem Solving & Decision Making	63-7	$7.95	
	Coaching & Counseling	68-8	$7.95	
	Ethics In Business	69-6	$7.95	
	Understanding Organizational Change	71-8	$7.95	
	Project Management	75-0	$7.95	
	Risk Taking	76-9	$7.95	
	Managing Organizational Change	80-7	$7.95	
	Working Together In A Multi-Cultural Organization	85-8	$7.95	
	Selecting And Working With Consultants	87-4	$7.95	
	PERSONNEL MANAGEMENT			
	Your First Thirty Days: A Professional Image in a New Job	003-5	$7.95	
	Office Management: A Guide To Productivity	005-1	$7.95	
	Men and Women: Partners at Work	009-4	$7.95	
	Effective Performance Appraisals—Revised	11-4	$7.95	
	Quality Interviewing—Revised	13-0	$7.95	
	Personal Counseling	14-9	$7.95	
	Attacking Absenteeism	042-6	$7.95	
	New Employee Orientation	46-7	$7.95	
	Professional Excellence For Secretaries	52-1	$7.95	
	Guide To Affirmative Action	54-8	$7.95	
	Writing A Human Resources Manual	70-X	$7.95	
	Winning at Human Relations	86-6	$7.95	
	WELLNESS			
	Mental Fitness	15-7	$7.95	
	Wellness in the Workplace	020-5	$7.95	
	Personal Wellness	021-3	$7.95	

Quantity	Title		
	WELLNESS (CONTINUED)		
	Preventing Job Burnout	23-8	
	Job Performance and Chemical Dependency	27-0	$7.95
	Overcoming Anxiety	029-9	$7.95
	Productivity at the Workstation	041-8	$7.95
	COMMUNICATIONS		
	Technical Writing In The Corporate World	004-3	$7.95
	Giving and Receiving Criticism	023-X	$7.95
	Effective Presentation Skills	24-6	$7.95
	Better Business Writing—Revised	25-4	$7.95
	Business Etiquette And Professionalism	032-9	$7.95
	The Business Of Listening	34-3	$7.95
	Writing Fitness	35-1	$7.95
	The Art Of Communicating	45-9	$7.95
	Technical Presentation Skills	55-6	$7.95
	Making Humor Work	61-0	$7.95
	Visual Aids In Business	77-7	$7.95
	Speed-Reading In Business	78-5	$7.95
	Publicity Power	82-3	$7.95
	Influencing Others	84-X	$7.95
	SELF-MANAGEMENT		
	Attitude: Your Most Priceless Possession-Revised	011-6	$7.95
	Personal Time Management	22-X	$7.95
	Successful Self-Management	26-2	$7.95
	Balancing Home And Career—Revised	035-3	$7.95
	Developing Positive Assertiveness	38-6	$7.95
	The Telephone And Time Management	53-X	$7.95
	Memory Skills In Business	56-4	$7.95
	Developing Self-Esteem	66-1	$7.95
	Creativity In Business	67-X	$7.95
	Managing Personal Change	74-2	$7.95
	Stop Procrastinating: Get To Work!	88-2	$7.95
	CUSTOMER SERVICE/SALES TRAINING		
	Sales Training Basics—Revised	02-5	$7.95
	Restaurant Server's Guide—Revised	08-4	$7.95
	Telephone Courtesy And Customer Service	18-1	$7.95
	Effective Sales Management	031-0	$7.95
	Professional Selling	42-4	$7.95
	Customer Satisfaction	57-2	$7.95
	Telemarketing Basics	60-2	$7.95
	Calming Upset Customers	65-3	$7.95
	Quality At Work	72-6	$7.95
	Managing Quality Customer Service	83-1	$7.95
	Quality Customer Service—Revised	95-5	$7.95
	SMALL BUSINESS AND FINANCIAL PLANNING		
	Understanding Financial Statements	022-1	$7.95
	Marketing Your Consulting Or Professional Services	40-8	$7.95

Quantity	Title	Code #	Price	Amount
	SMALL BUSINESS AND FINANCIAL PLANNING (CONTINUED)			
	Starting Your New Business	44-0	$7.95	
	Personal Financial Fitness—Revised	89-0	$7.95	
	Financial Planning With Employee Benefits	90-4	$7.95	
	BASIC LEARNING SKILLS			
	Returning To Learning: Getting Your G.E.D.	002-7	$7.95	
	Study Skills Strategies—Revised	05-X	$7.95	
	The College Experience	007-8	$7.95	
	Basic Business Math	024-8	$7.95	
	Becoming An Effective Tutor	028-0	$7.95	
	CAREER PLANNING			
	Career Discovery	07-6	$7.95	
	Effective Networking	030-2	$7.95	
	Preparing for Your Interview	033-7	$7.95	
	Plan B: Protecting Your Career	48-3	$7.95	
	I Got the Job!	59-9	$7.95	
	RETIREMENT			
	Personal Financial Fitness—Revised	89-0	$7.95	
	Financial Planning With Employee Benefits	90-4	$7.95	

OTHER CRISP INC. BOOKS

Quantity	Title	Code #	Price	Amount
	Desktop Publishing	001-9	$ 5.95	
	Stepping Up To Supervisor	11-8	$13.95	
	The Unfinished Business Of Living: Helping Aging Parents	19-X	$12.95	
	Managing Performance	23-7	$19.95	
	Be True To Your Future: A Guide To Life Planning	47-5	$13.95	
	Up Your Productivity	49-1	$10.95	
	Comfort Zones: Planning Your Future 2/e	73-4	$13.95	
	Copyediting 2/e	94-7	$18.95	
	Recharge Your Career	027-2	$12.95	
	Practical Time Management	275-4	$13.95	

VIDEO TITLE*

Quantity	Video Title*	Code #	Preview	Purchase	Amount
	Attitude: Your Most Priceless Possession	012-4	$25.00	$395.00	
	Quality Customer Service	013-2	$25.00	$395.00	
	Team Building	014-2	$25.00	$395.00	
	Job Performance & Chemical Dependency	015-9	$25.00	$395.00	
	Better Business Writing	016-7	$25.00	$395.00	
	Comfort Zones	025-6	$25.00	$395.00	
	Creativity in Business	036-1	$25.00	$395.00	
	Motivating at Work	037-X	$25.00	$395.00	
	Calming Upset Customers	040-X	$25.00	$395.00	
	Balancing Home and Career	048-5	$25.00	$395.00	
	Stress and Mental Fitness	049-3	$25.00	$395.00	

(*Note: All tapes are VHS format. Video package includes five books and a Leader's Guide.)

Total Books	
Less Discount (5 or more different books 20% sampler)	
Total Videos	
Less Discount (purchase of 3 or more videos earn 20%)	
Shipping ($3.50 per video, $.50 per book)	
California Tax (California residents add 7%)	
TOTAL	

☐ Send volume discount information.   ☐ Please send me a catalog.

☐ Please charge the following credit card   ☐ Mastercard   ☐ VISA   ☐ AMEX

Account No. _____   Name (as appears on card) _____

Ship to: _____   Bill to: _____

_____   _____

_____   _____

_____   _____

Phone number: _____   P.O. # _____

All orders except those with a P.O.# must be prepaid.
For more information Call (415) 949-4888 or FAX (415) 949-1610.

BUSINESS REPLY
FIRST CLASS   PERMIT NO. 884   LOS ALTOS, CA

POSTAGE WILL BE PAID BY ADDRESSEE

Crisp Publications, Inc.
95 First Street
Los Altos, CA 94022

NO POSTAGE
NECESSARY
IF MAILED
IN THE
UNITED STATES